the 2014 SOMERSET FLOODS

Laura Zaky &
Jason Bryant

HALSGROVE

First published in Great Britain in 2014

British Library Cataloguing-in-Publication Data
A CIP record for this title is available from the British Library

ISBN 978 0 85704 252 1

HALSTAR
Halsgrove House,
Ryelands Business Park,
Bagley Road, Wellington, Somerset TA21 9PZ
Tel: 01823 653777   Fax: 01823 216796
email: sales@halsgrove.com

Part of the Halsgrove group of companies
Information on all Halsgrove titles is available at: www.halsgrove.com

Printed in China by Everbest Printing Co Ltd

Introduction

Much of the UK suffered dreadful weather from Christmas 2013 and on well into 2014. However, in Somerset the situation was perhaps worse than anywhere else, with seemingly relentless rain causing the flood waters to rise inexorably until villages were cut off and thousands of acres of farmland lay underwater. The plight of the Somerset Levels and Moors really hit the public consciousness when HRH Prince Charles visited the flood-affected areas on 4 February. His visit gave a tremendous boost to desperate communities and also highlighted the relief efforts being undertaken and what was still required to be done.

It was at this point that Laura Zaky became involved with FLAG – Flooding on the Levels Action Group – as a volunteer logistics coordinator, and joined forces with local professional freelance photographer Jason Bryant. Together they recorded as much as they could, not only of the remarkable scenes of devastation but also of the tremendous behind-the-scenes efforts to help.

What follows is not a day-to-day diary of these desperate months, but rather a collage of images that tell a remarkable story of human resilience in the face of almost overwhelming elemental force.

Photographers await the arrival of HRH Prince Charles in Muchelney, 4 February 2014.

HRH Prince Charles' boat was guided into
the village by the Avon and Somerset Police.

HRH Prince Charles waves to onlookers at Mulchney.
Little did he know there was worse to come.

Prince Charles en route
to Thorney.

Below: HRH Prince Charles being interviewed. Later in the day, a private aside
about the way the floods were being handled caught national attention.

The 'everyday' story of the floods: daily lives on hold, journeys taking endless time to do routine shopping or school runs, emergency services diverted from regular duty.

STOP THE FLOODING

"With our land submerged it soon became apparent that our house was next. We'd asked for help and no-one came. We were on our own. The social media pages of FLAG (our Facebook group) became the go-to community resource for help. As houses and farms like friend James Winslade's pictured below became overwhelmed by the flooding, the online community suddenly became an army of real-life volunteers, we were there for one another and together we found strength. Armed with nothing more than smartphones and laptops we somehow managed to coordinate sandbagging, livestock evacuations, not to mention possessions, pets and even cars! People volunteered their time, companies donated goods and the general public rallied behind us. The response was phenomenal. We also somehow managed to keep campaigning for the rivers to be dredged even though we had been evacuated from our homes. This is only the beginning, we will continue to campaign for better water management throughout the Somerset Levels and catchment to try and ensure flooding of this scale doesn't happen again."

Gavin Sadler, Moorland resident,
FLAG flood campaigner

Above: Gavin Sadler, assisting in the evacuation of West Yeo Farm, talks on the phone to farmer James Winslade *(right).*

Opposite: The evacuation of cattle from James Winslade's West Yeo Farm.

Still rising, the scene at West Yeo Farm.

"The events of 2014 will be forever etched in my mind. FLAG started out as a group of concerned residents worried about the mismanagement of our waterways, of which I was one, but very quickly evolved into an emergency service that faced a near apocalyptic situation when the floodwater over-whelmed homes, farms and businesses. Personally I got involved because I have lived in this area for my whole life and I can see it being ruined by neglect and mismanagement of the waterways and rivers. I wanted to help my friends and the community save our homes and livelihoods. What is now clear is that now the emergency phase is over there is still a lot of work to do. This should never have happened and was a true man-made disaster. I will fight to ensure that we never suffer a flood like this again."

Rebecca Horsington

James Winslade's cattle at West Yeo Farm.

Below: Farmer Jon King's tractor having slid into a ditch at West Yeo Farm evacuating cattle.

The evacuation of cattle from West Yeo Farm near Moorland.

James Winslade directs operations to evacuate cattle.

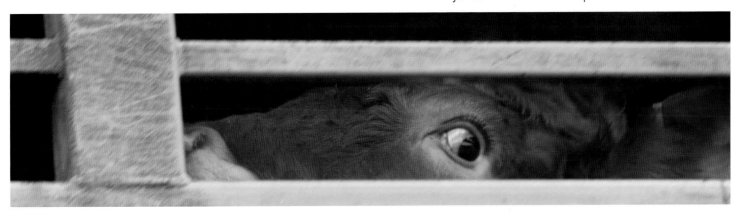

Below: Rebecca Horsington who through Facebook helped to organise the rescue of 550 beef cattle from West Yeo Farm.

Devastation at West Yeo Farm.

A cameraman hitches a lift. *Below:* The only way to travel!

Nick Clegg visits Langport.

Left: Nigel Farage in floodwater at Burrowbridge.

Overleaf: The view from Burrow Mump.

Above and left: 40 Commando came to help sandbag to secure homes in Moorland from the rising tides.

Longload Bridge. *Below:* Farmer Jon King surveys the damage in East Harptree.

ROAD
CLOSED

Above and left: The bridge at Burrowbridge.

Opposite: Beauty in the face of devastation.
Sunrise over floodwater near Glastonbury

Below: Returning with shopping.

Pump action!

Burrow Mump car park. *Below left:* A361 to Taunton – boats only. *Below right:* Jason Bryant returns from wading out towards Saltmoor.

Top left: Combined force effort to rescue 15 Basset hounds, 2 cross breeds, 16 cats and residents from West Yeo organized by Helen Toye FLAG Animal Co-ordinator with Heavens Gate Rescue Centre helping to transport the animals. FLAG helped get all the crates that were needed for such a big rescue.

Above: Jim Winkworth delivering hay to a flood-affected farm at Burrowbridge.

Left: Lovingly known as 'Pete's Marina', here in Burrowbridge a boat and pontoon were moored overnight. The sun is setting over the flooded moors.

The Winkworth Way, named after the landlord of the King Alfred at Burrowbridge, Jim Winkworth. This river path was a lifeline and volunteers worked hard to re-enforce the banks and keep the path open so that residents from either end of Burrowbridge remained connected and had access to their homes. Volunteers and residents used this to wheelbarrow supply runs to a 4x4 at the other end.

Tanya and Jay serving refreshments outside the Kind Alfred to volunteers.

Matt, Marie, tractor Tom and PCSO Georgie in Moorland on a sandbag run.

Below: Getting a warm drink at Derelict House, FLAG HQ, Moorland.

Left: A volunteer from the charity Khalsa Aid next to an Environment Agency van in Burrowbridge.

Below: Securing the river path to the Saltmoor Pump.

Opposite: A Vanheck team from Holland with 40 Commando securing a bund.

Glastonbury.

Jet ski champion Joel Doorbar in action.

Below: Yes, it's official! A Great White shark has been spotted in floodwater near Glastonbury – or could it be a piece of wood shaped like a tail fin on the end of a stick put there as a prank?

Welcome to
SOMERSET
Erected by Somerset County Council in the year
of the Golden Jubilee of Queen Elizabeth II 2002
Twinned with Atlantis

"Once the plight of the Somerset levels had come to national attention in February 2014, the amount of data that FLAG Somerset were faced with, quickly overwhelmed them. I helped FLAG by taking the existing old-fashioned spreadsheets full of offers of help, and put them into Google Drive. From that moment on, we could share them and work collaberatively on them with anyone on the face of the planet who had an internet browser and a Gmail account. We could get people to input their own offers directly into the spreadsheet using a 'form'. We could put that 'form' onto any website we had access to. We didn't have to maintain anything (no servers, no databases, nothing) because it was all in Google's infrastructure. If I were going to advise anybody on how to prepare in case they might find themselves in the same situation, I'd get them to find out what is freely and widely available on the internet. Particularly from Google."

Alistair Munro, Data Specialist and Flag Volunteer

Donation from Asda – 1,600 pairs of waders unloaded by volunteers. 20 people turned up to help unload the 40ft lorry at 9pm at Junction 24.

"The Somerset Levels flooding continued to escalate through Febraury, and during this time I began getting involved with more volunteers sorting and distributing the donations that were initially sent in to Britannia Lanes. After a couple days it became apparent that the scale of the devastation warranted a larger and more permanent base for this critical task. I spoke to my boss at work and was offered a warehouse at an EDF property at Junction 24. Three days later we were up and running as a Flood Aid distribution centre.

For the next three months my team and I co-ordinated the volunteering effort and running of the centre, during which time the warehouse evolved many times responding to the dynamic situation, eventually becoming known as the Somerset Flood Relief Centre (SFRC) for those affected and the army of volunteers supporting the community. Many individuals, organisations, agencies, businesses large and small supported the centre and we in turn supported many families that were evacuated with essential supplies including clothing, bedding, food, drink and many other essentials including emotional support in our 'safe space' café. We also supplied all of the families, volunteers and organisations with the required protective clothing and essential equipment to keep the emergency response moving and attempt to minimise the devastation caused. Following the emergency response, we also supported the families and volunteers with all the essentials for the initial recovery stages and the clean up of the community."

Paul Blackmore *(second from left)*

Stuart Smith *(right)* joined FLAG on the 8 February and at the time of publication had done in excess of 100 days, working initially in Moorland with Marie, Matt, Sam and Tom helping flooded residents get their belongings from houses, and cars from drive-ways. If the car started on the drive they moved it using a tractor and trailer and then pontoons. The teams grew and split to do different tasks throughout the flooded areas; as more help came from the authorities the FLAG teams advised and guided the way with their on-the-ground knowledge and relationships with residents.

"In the beginning I was taking 400 calls a day and we were sending out #FLAGSHOUTS [Facebook messages] in abundance for many different things. Thank you each and everyone who answered our calls for help"

Stuart Smith, FLAG Logistics Co-ordinator Moorland

Pumps at Moorland. *Below:* Pipes at Dunball Sluice.

37

Makeshift signs popping up, this one near Muchelney.

Below: The road to Muchelney.

"The starkness of the news from Devon, Somerset and the Thames Valley that due to terrible storms, people and animals were having to be evacuated. The ground-swell of sympathy, coming together, ingenuity and organisation from the population and offers and acts of help, most generous. The indignity, on hearing the evidence that the Somerset Levels flooding was partly due to mismanagement by the authorities. The desire to work to mimimise future adverse events of this kind, to bring comfort to the affected people, thanks to the volunteers and recovery for the wider area."

Alan Cook, FLAG volunteer

Counting the costs – from wasted sandbags to dead sheep.

Right: Burrow Mump.

The DUKW (colloquially known as Duck) is a six-wheel-drive modification of the 2-ton capacity "deuce" trucks used by the U.S. military and Royal Marines during the Second World War. DUKWs were later used as tourist craft in marine environments and now the Somerset Floods. This was valuable to help get supplies to cut-off homes in Moorland.

View into Moorland from the inside of the BvS.

A BvS Vehicle ran in Moorland connecting the flooded neighbours with their cars and lives outside the floods, as well as getting helpers in, and people to their homes to rescue their belongings and supplies to those cut off by the floods. Lovingly known as 'The Ninky-Nonk'.

"I only came to Moorland to deliver some food to an elderly couple whose house was surrounded by water. I stayed for the day to help sandbag, I saw the devastation that had engulfed the village, and saw I could make a difference. I've been up to my neck in water, pushing a pontoon in freezing water, I've cleared houses of sodden carpets, beds, furniture, I've emptied freezers and fridges that have been underwater for weeks. Cleared sandbags, ripped down walls and plaster, taken apart people's homes when the water took apart their lives. But more than anything, by helping I've helped make people's lives a bit better, and even more than that I've made people smile. I'm proud to work with such an amazing group of volunteers, people from all walks of life, and every age range.

Dawn Hackney, Asda Security Manager, Taunton

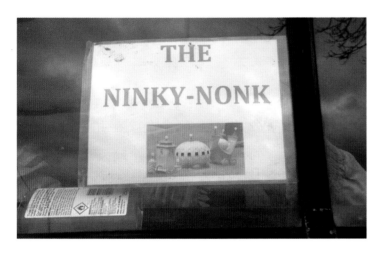

Mr Bristow *(below right)* secured his home in Moorland from the floods using a sandbag bund and also dug a hole in his dining room to prevent his home flooding. Dawn Hackney *(below left)* has just dropped off some beer for him.

A FLAG rescue – a bear, now lovingly known as Floodsie. He was rescued from a pontoon in Moorland by Morgan and Oska Zaky. He has gone on to be a celebrity with many outfits being made for him including his own set of waders! He has been on his travels including meeting the cast of *Hollyoaks* at a flood charity football match in Street.

Sam Notaro protected his house in Moorland with a huge bund. *Below:* Tractoring in sandbags to Moorland.

The heart of Moorland – which ever way you turn it's flooded.

Above: The bund at the top of Church Lane, Moorland.

Inset: The BvS taking volunteers and residents back to the other side of Moorland.

Angela Greenway became the 'Arkwright Stores' for the 14 homes in Moorland beyond the bund. Her conservatory is shown stocked with supplies for her flooded neighbours. Pictured with Justine Baker, Somerset County Councillor.

A garden shed collapsed and broken by the flood water.

Fire & Rescue crew fully kitted-up in dry suits taking a walk through Moorland, checking the depth as the waters start to go down.

Below: Two cars unable to be rescued with the flood lines clearly marked.

The Toledo that famously did not sell on ebay.

Mitsubishi Motors UK donated 2 L200s for FLAG logistics teams run by Tim Holmes and Stuart Smith, to use in Burrowbridge and Moorland.

Left: Royal Marines in Burrowbridge going out to a rescue at Moorland/ West Yeo.

The A361 at Burrowbridge.

The view from Burrow Mump.

View from Glastonbury Tor. A fire engine making it's way to Glastonbury through the flood waters on the Butleigh Road.

Returning from a rescue at Burrowbridge. *Below:* Avon and Somerset Police head to Muchelney.

Matt Baker from 'Countryfile' teams up with the Devon & Somerset Fire, Water, Flood Rescue.

Below: The Devon & Somerset Fire, Water, Flood Rescue team out on surveillance on the River Parrett near Moorland.

The River Brue breaks its banks near Glastonbury.

Left: Pumping out flooded fields near Burrowbridge.

"I have friends in Fordgate whom I have known for over 35 years, I wanted to help, they were holding their own as they were on higher ground. Through social media I found FLAG (Flooding on the Levels Action Group). I met with some members. I helped in my spare time as a volunteer logistics co-ordinator in Burrowbridge and Moorland working with Tim, Stuart and the authorities to help deliver solutions to the daily changing needs; this evolved into photographing and documenting activities of flooded neighbours and volunteers."

Laura Zaky, FLAG Logistics Co-ordinator

Photographer Jason Bryant pictured in Mulchelney.

"I could see on Facebook that people weren't getting any help whilst the waters were rising, so I thought why don't I get out there and help. So with a few other people I organised a sand-bagging operation to help save people's homes. Soon enough the water was too high for sandbags so our intentions moved on to rescuing cars, pets and belongings, this continued for about two months. Once the water had receded we moved onto clearing up homes and gardens. This was all made possible by a brilliant group of volunteers."

Tim Holmes, FLAG Logistics, Burrowbridge

Circa 240 tones of sand was bagged over the weekend of 8-9 February 2014 organised by Tim Holmes; here was the makeshift sand bag maker. This helped save people's homes and secure the river bank on the Winkworth Way in Burrowbridge. This sand was kindly donated by S. Morris, Champions and Khalsa Aid. Many, many hands helped.

Right: Tools used to secure the river paths with mulch. Glastonbury Festival were contacted to take their advice about mud and how to deal with making it safe to walk on.

A disabled child saved from his home in the floods.

Mr Donaldson *(below)* stayed on his property *(left)*. He's just come into Burrowbridge to collect supplies for himself and the animals. Also taking the dog for a walk!

Keith Mansfield *(grey top)* and Stuart take a moment on Burrowbridge.

Below: Police Community Point where locals catch up on the day's events.

Tim Holmes, Burrowbridge and Stuart Smith, Moorland Logistics, out on a check-up on the A361. *Below:* River Parrett, Burrowbridge.

Burrowbridge. Still flooded, the road from Moorland just passable from Saltmoor by 4x4.

Below: Police cordon at the top of Huntworth Lane, Huntworth.

The Moorland triangle Community Police Point.

Below: After the waters had receded the Community Police Point was sited at Moorland Village Hall.

Moorland churchyard.

Craig Roberston keeps an
eye on flooding next to
Shepton Mallet Prison.

Vauxhall Corsa abandoned in Burrowbridge.

Below: Ladybirds take refuge as a sculpted boy keeps his head and shoulders above the flood waters.

Press and camera crews gather to get an interview. *Below:* Pontoon coming in to land while a TV interview takes place.

David Woodland *(left)*, Adam Gray *(bottom left)*
and Matilda Temperley *(bottom right)*.

Everyday life saw the Press and TV crews documenting and interviewing the locals and volunteers in the midst of the activities in and around the floods. Many were on TV or in the papers at some point. It was an intrinsic part of keeping the story alive, in addition to the work of the social media group, FLAG (Flooding on the Levels Action Group) that grew swiftly from 600 to now in excess of 12,000 strong.

Khalsa Aid: In 1999, Ravi *(pictured far right)* from the Thames Valley, founded the Sikh humanitarian charity Khalsa Aid. It has been on missions to Albania, the Philippines, Haiti and in 2014 he spent over two months helping the worst affected Somerset flood areas. Ravi's help with financial aid and teams of helpers including his sons and a steady supply of samosas. Somerset found a new friend.

"I was born in Singapore, grew up in Punjab, travelled the world and of all the places on earth.... I lost my heart in a small English village, Burrowbridge. Life can be so mysterious and yet wonderful."

Ravi Singh

Khalsa Aid deliver from the Thames Valley...

"I feel really proud to have been there right at the start of the flood relief. As soon as there was a fear of properties flooding I used the FLAG Facebook group to bring together a small team of people co-ordinating offers and requests for help for sandbagging, transport, housing, equipment and much much more. The moment there was the need to evacuate animals and people we were ready to assist where the authorities could not. It was a manic February, organising and leading this organisation as well as working closely with Somerset County Council and Silver Command. It was well worth it as it paved the way for some amazing volunteering work and has started the discussion of what role the authorities have to play in events like the Somerset floods."

Alfred Van Pelt pictured above with Ravi Singh

Pipes for the diesel pipeline to keep the pump at Saltmoor running. *Below:* The Forces join for a brief discussion on the day's events.

Royal Marines were deployed to help reinforce flood defences. 18 Marines from 40 Commando, near Taunton, helped with a major sandbagging operation at Stanmoor Bank near Burrowbridge. They put out nearly 1000 sandbags along a 1-2km stretch of the retaining wall which was being reinforced to prevent overtopping by flood waters.

"We've had the support of the military on standby throughout this major incident. Staff from many different agencies had worked tirelessly to fill and put out sandbags. They were working flat out and Royal Marines manpower was deployed to bring fresh energy and extra support which was very much appreciated."

Chief Superintendent Caroline Peters,
Gold Commander

Securing the area and making a new pedestrian walkway for flooded residents to get access to Saltmoor/Burrowbridge.

Royal Engineers working to secure the diesel pipeline as a second measure to keep Saltmoor pump working.

Below: A very large specialist boat crane as a third measure to keep fuel to the Saltmoor pump.

The Royal Engineers checking data with the police.

Jim Winkworth checking he can still get his
quad through the gap to the pathway to
Saltmoor now the fuel pipeline is in situ

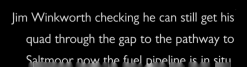

Royal Marines with their boats as a fourth measure to get diesel to the Saltmoor pump across the River Parrett. Luckily neither the pump or boats were needed.

Jim Winkworth along with his wife Sally run the King Alfred Pub in Burrowbridge. During the floods it became the hub of comunications and the local shop, post office, volunteers café etc. for the flood afftected, volunteers, combined forces, flood tourists, MPs, TV and Press alike. Before the floods, before the people, this was a quiet community who enjoyed the weekend visitors and holidaymakers and all the locals. Now, Jim who helped his friends and neighbours since New Year's Eve said "It's so much more a community now we all know each other not just a hello or a wave." Jim helped with getting food and supplies to people cut off. Helped people get to work and home again. Worked all hours in all weathers with other locals to save their community. As a core mamber of FLAG the action group to campaign for better water management throughout the Somerset Levels and catchment. Jim *(top right)* being interviewed on Burrowbridge. Jim said "It restores your belief in mankind and humanity." Now very good friends with Ravi Singh from Khalsa Aid they work on projects together widening the Burrowbridge family.

Many of the staff deployed to work daily at Burrowbridge and Moorland lent a helping hand to the distribution of mulch along the river bank – hundreds of wheel barrows back and forth. All ages helped out.

The King Alfred Pub at Burrowbridge was the hub of operations from the beginning. Here the volunteers help spruce up the front in quieter times, post main crisis as a thank you to Sally and Jim.

"I first got directly involved in the flooding when I took over managing the humanitarian boat service to Muchelney. I will never forget how I felt when I first arrived at Langport and saw the acres of water, it was powerful and shocking. It was great to be able to have close links with the community and help meet their needs whilst they were cut off. I was one of the first local authority officers to get into the flood and into a flooded resident's home, a sight I will never forget. I then volunteered to work at Burrowbridge helping the volunteers and the community; it was a very rewarding experience as I knew I was making a real difference at a time when everyone was going through such a stressful time trying to save homes from being flooded. It struck me how effective local authorities can be when we work like this; on the ground, face to face and often shoulder to shoulder with the people of Somerset, it can be such a good way to serve them at their time of need."

Barry James Strategic Commissioning Manager, Community Infrastructure Somerset County Council *(centre),* Jill Shortland County Councilor *(left)* and Stuart Smith *(right)* SEV in Moorland.

The Vanheck team out at Moorland. *Below:* Event scaffold steps and gantry so residents can access the river path past the Saltmoor pumping station.

An impressive row of eight massive pumps from the Netherlands, form the heart of a new mobile pumping station that became operational near Dunball Sluice on 13 February 2014. The temporary station is pumping flood water from the King's Sedgemoor Drain into the River Parrett at a rate of 56,000 m3 every hour. The Dutch firm Vanheck Group brought the equipment over from the Netherlands and managed to get the massive pumps operational in just a few days. Company director Jeroen van Heck said: "It has not been an easy job as we had to use high cranes to lift the pumps into place. For safety reasons, we had to stop work on a number of occasions." In addition to the extra pumping capacity, the temporary pumping station enabled the Environment Agency and Somerset County Council to continue their flood relief efforts, regardless of the tide on the River Parrett. An impressive convoy of 30 trailers drove in the pumps and the necessary support equipment from the Netherlands. Vanheck had a total of 20 pumps in operation on the Somerset Levels. It is the biggest flood recovery operation in the history of the Dutch company.

Right: Prime Minister David Cameron vists Moorland following the floods pictured with MP Ian Liddell-Grainger and the Environment Agency team.
Below: RAF Chinook.
Below right: Chairman of Moorland Village Hall Julian Taylor with the temporary Moorland Village Hall.

Debris in a field at Burrowbridge. *Below:* Beautiful reflections, Polsham near Wells.

Burrowbridge now by the sea. *Below:* A diver from Street sub aqua club takes a dip at Burrowbridge.

Burrowbridge before and after the water went.

Moorland before and after the water went.

Daily meetings held with Armed Forces, Police, Somerset County Council, FLAG Logistics team, EA and local residents. These meetings were valuable and helped keep communication very strong and co-ordination more effective.

"We just did what we had to do". **Heather Venn** FLAG Chairman

A property in Moorland before the waters rose over one foot more.

Below left: Jill Shortland, County Councillor, discussing the requirements to help this uninsured family get back in their home. So many people were uninsured or under insured. With the generosity of businesses, labourers and Somerset Emergency Volunteers these people will get the help they need.

Below: A ditch on the way from Moorland to Burrowbridge with a lost straw bale and the water tide marks.

Drying out flood affected homes. *Below:* The ruins of belongings in a skip, now contaminated waste.

So why did I do this? When Typhoon Hiyan hit my family's homeland in the Philippines I knew I could not help as they were so far away. I knew in Somerset I could help. Supporting the people and their homes was a massive priority and I could not stand by and watch people suffering. I had many experiences on the Somerset Levels, from dealing with the emotions of saving people's properties by sand bagging, retrieving and saving people's belongings, bringing essential aid, and just talking to people etc. I was even given the opportunity by Tim to co-ordinate volunteer objectives on the ground during the flooding period. I took a step back on one of these days and was humbled and awe inspired at what I witnessed. People in the community and volunteers, none of whom knew each other pulled together, working side by side helping each other, building sandbag defences, wheel barrowing wood chip, making lunch for people and just talking to each other and keeping each other's spirits up. Ultimately how the human spirit drives through helping each other in times of crisis.

Mark Rosalis, FLAG Fundraising and Events team

Uncle Tony's in Fordgate getting measured up for a new kitchen. *Below:* Surveyor checking out the water damage.

Stuart and some of the team at the Moorland HQ. *Below:* Volunteers unloading debris from flood affected homes.

Stuart Smith, with the help of Sadie Foster, has gone on to set up Somerset Emergency Volunteers; they moved their HQ to Burrowbridge School in late May 2014 and continued to help the flood affected residents in collaboration with Somerset County Council. Stuart said "I will not leave until all the residents have a home to live in." He is very thankful for all of the help and support that has been given over this challenging period. Sadie always with a smile on her face has made a formidable team with Stuart.

Right: The *One Show* visits.

Left and below: Junction 24 warehouse which housed donations for those affected by the floods.

"Life changing, soul searching but Somerset pulled together and became a force to behold"

Helen Toye, FLAG Animal Rescue Co-ordinator

Tesco deliver household packs for flood affected people, volunteers help unpack the lorry loads.

Mark Rosales and the volunteers out in Currymoor helping Keith get his home and firewood business back together.

"From the loss and devastation when the floods receded, what remained and formed was a friendship that was to see the community rebuild, not just in bricks and mortar but within the support of communities and neighbours alike, a refinement that has seen the Levels' future and its vulnerability debated and we shall always hope on the path to now being restored. What brought me to the Levels you ask, its beauty – the knowing that this is a part of the country that we could not afford to lose, and basically there was a need that I could help be met, I couldn't always give money I need not have, but now my daughter was secure in pre-school, the time I had, I have given – because after all if you can't help those in need when that is needed, what neighbour are we to them, and when I travel through the villages next year what a smile I shall have, knowing that not only villagers and nature have been restored but that the future of the Levels will be there for generations to come. Somerset is not a county without its villages and to lose part of its farming industry and area of natural interest, what will we be left to be locally proud of?"

Lorri Bee Volunteer

A static home for one West Yeo resident to live in whilst their home is dried and repaired.

Looking out at the daffodils accross the road, this West Yeo resident remembers how she and her friend, 15 Basset hounds, 2 cross breed dogs and 16 cats were rescued.

"I remember getting off the amphibious vehicle at Burrowbridge to be greeted by you, Laura and Helen you gave us both a big FLAG hug. Then took us to get supplies for us and our animals at the King Alfred Pub. We were overwhelmed by the generosity of everyone, Thank you so very much. I'm glad to be home and that it is all over."

"I remember at the beginning when we came for a meal at the King Alfred and you, Laura cheered us up so much. The floods have torn a community apart but are now partly re-joining. For ourselves we sit in a static caravan in the drive watching our house slowly being rebuilt. It is hard, stressful and life changing but I say that the caravan is, for now, our home, and the house is our project It helps us keep our sanity. I also am pleased when we can have a 'bonus' day. For instance, the day the loss adjuster approved my new kitchen and duck egg blue cooker. Brill.

Sue Crocker, Fordgate flooded resident

The pump pipes dismantled and ready to go home.
Also tonnes of hardcore to be redistributed.

The Pontoon & Dock
Company Ltd
QUALITY MARINA EQUIPMENT
Tel: 0845 1080420
www.pontoonanddock.com

Dave from Talent.uk.com Saltmoor, Burrowbridge was kept in business with the help of FLAG volunteers ferrying their deliveries by boat, pontoon and 4x4. Here they are making their post connection outside the King Alfred Pub, Burrowbridge, which was one of the first times they were able to break through with a 4x4.

The Basket Centre following the floods at Burrowbridge. *Below:* Flooded fields near Shepton Mallet.

Environment Agency taking stock of the devastation. Teams from all over the country came to help with their varied knowledge of flooding, telemetry and water management. They were suprised at the level of flooding – "seeing is believing" one manager said. "It is very useful for us to feed this back. Being on the ground brings it home." The EA were very helpful in supplying maps and regular updates so that FLAG Logistics could make sure all homes had been visited and aware of sluice gate and pump times.

The Derelict House. FLAG HQ with volunteers getting ready to go out to help.

Dredging begins following the floods.

Flooded farm land near
Shepton Mallet.

The view from Burrow
Mump following the floods.

Tim Holmes and Jess at the King Alfred.

Inset: James Winslade and Jon King following the floods.

Rebecca Horsington and Bryony Sadler of FLAG meet minister Owen Patterson at the Royal Bath and West Show.

James Winslade of West Yeo Farm meets the Duchess of Cornwall at the Royal Bath and West Show.

On this and following pages, a montage of images
that encapsulate the varied aspects of the floods.

The mounted police on patrol at Burrowbridge.

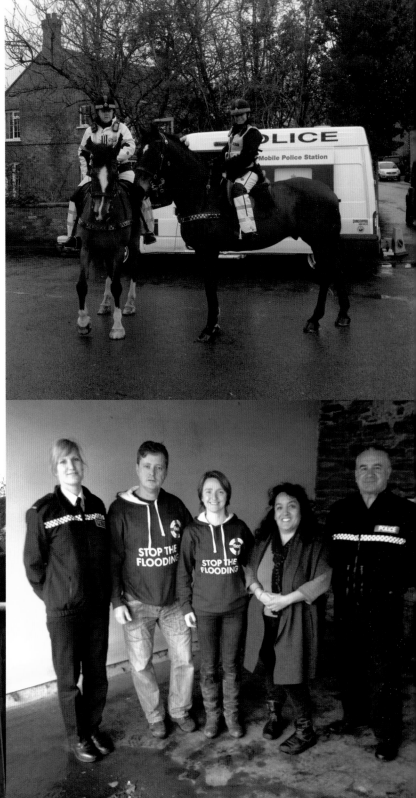

Below left: Matt Cardy, freelance and editorial press photographer, taking a ride on the BvS in to Moorland.

Below right: The FLAG communication team, Alfred, Stephanie and Laura at Silver Command with their liaison officers.

Glastonbury Tor.

Fog on the Somerset Levels. *Below:* Godney.

Jason Bryant photographs Matildia Temperley.

FLAG abseil down County Hall. *Below left:* Martin. *Below right:* Ian Liddell-Grainger MP stopped for a picture.

As the waters receded two ladies take a moment for a chat on the bench in Moorland churchyard.

People from all walks of life coming to help, putting their lives on hold. Donations flooding in nationwide from socks to food to waders companies offering their catalogues. True British Spirit!